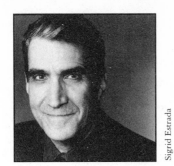

Sigrid Estrada

# Robert Pinsky
## *Jersey Rain*

ROBERT PINSKY, United States Poet Laureate 1997–2000, has received the William Carlos Williams Prize, the Lenore Marshall Poetry Prize, and the *Los Angeles Times* Book Award. He has won critical acclaim for his collected poems *The Figured Wheel* (1996), his translation *The Inferno of Dante* (1994), and his guidebook *The Sounds of Poetry* (1998). He is poetry editor of *Slate* and a contributor to television's *The NewsHour with Jim Lehrer*, and he teaches at Boston University.

# By Robert Pinsky

*Poetry*
Sadness And Happiness (1975)
An Explanation of America (1979)
History of My Heart (1984)
The Want Bone (1990)
The Figured Wheel (1996)

*Prose*
Landor's Poetry (1968)
The Situation of Poetry (1977)
Poetry and the World (1988)
The Sounds of Poetry (1998)

*Translations*
The Separate Notebooks, by Czeslaw Milosz (1983)
The Inferno of Dante (1994)

# Jersey Rain

# Jersey Rain

## Robert Pinsky

*Farrar, Straus and Giroux*

*New York*

Farrar, Straus and Giroux
19 Union Square West, New York 10003

Distributed in Canada by Douglas & McIntyre Ltd.
Printed in the United States of America
Published in 2000 by Farrar, Straus and Giroux
First paperback edition, 2001

Library of Congress Cataloging-in-Publication Data
Pinsky, Robert.
    Jersey rain / Robert Pinsky. — 1st ed.
        p.   cm.
    ISBN 0-374-52772-5 (pbk.)
    I. Title.
    PS3566.I54J47   2000
    811'.54—dc21                          99-44209

Designed by Jonathan D. Lippincott

Grateful acknowledgment is made to the editors of the magazines where the following poems appeared: "At the Worcester Museum" in *ARTnews*; "Biography," "Jersey Rain," and "Vessel" in *The Atlantic Monthly*; "A Phonebook Cover Hermes of the Nineteen-forties" in *The New Republic*; "The Green Piano," "Samurai Song," and "To Television" in *The New Yorker*; "ABC" and "A Prologue" in *The New York Review of Books*; "The Tragic Chorus" in *Ploughshares*; "Machines" in *Provincetown Arts*; "The Cycles," "In Memory of Congresswoman Barbara Jordan," "Porch Steps," "Song," "Summer in Saratoga Springs," and "To the Phoenix" in *Salmagundi*; "The Haunted Ruin" in *Slate*; "An Alphabet of My Dead," "Autumn Quartet," "Ode to Meaning," and "Steel Drum Variations" in *The Threepenny Review*; and "Victrola" in *Tikkun*.

*To*
*Louise Glück*
*and*
*Stephen Greenblatt*

# Contents

*Jersey Rain*

## Samurai Song

When I had no roof I made
Audacity my roof. When I had
No supper my eyes dined.

When I had no eyes I listened.
When I had no ears I thought.
When I had no thought I waited.

When I had no father I made
Care my father. When I had
No mother I embraced order.

When I had no friend I made
Quiet my friend. When I had no
Enemy I opposed my body.

When I had no temple I made
My voice my temple. I have
No priest, my tongue is my choir.

When I have no means fortune
Is my means. When I have
Nothing, death will be my fortune.

Need is my tactic, detachment
Is my strategy. When I had
No lover I courted my sleep.

## Vessel

What is this body as I fall asleep again?
What I pretended it was when I was small—

A crowded vessel, a starship or submarine
Dark in its dark element, a breathing hull,

Arms at the flanks, the engine heart and brain
Pulsing, feet pointed like a diver's, the whole

Resolutely diving through the oblivion
Of night with living cargo. O carrier shell

That keeps your trusting passengers from All:
Some twenty thousand times now you have gone

Out into blackness tireless as a seal,
Blind always as a log, but plunging on

Across the reefs of coral that scrape the keel—
O veteran immersed from toe to crown,

Buoy the population of the soul
Toward their destination before they drown.

## Ode to Meaning

Dire one and desired one,
Savior, sentencer—

In an old allegory you would carry
A chained alphabet of tokens:

Ankh Badge Cross.
Dragon,
Engraved figure guarding a hallowed intaglio,
Jasper kinema of legendary Mind,
Naked omphalos pierced
By quills of rhyme or sense, torah-like: unborn
Vein of will, xenophile
Yearning out of Zero.

Untrusting I court you. Wavering
I seek your face, I read
That Crusoe's knife
Reeked of you, that to defile you
The soldier makes the rabbi spit on the torah.
"I'll drown my book" says Shakespeare.

Drowned walker, revenant.
After my mother fell on her head, she became
More than ever your sworn enemy. She spoke
Sometimes like a poet or critic of forty years later.
Or she spoke of the world as Thersites spoke of the heroes,
"I think they have swallowed one another. I
Would laugh at that miracle."

You also in the laughter, warrior angel:
Your helmet the zodiac, rocket-plumed
Your spear the beggar's finger pointing to the mouth
Your heel planted on the serpent Formulation
Your face a vapor, the wreath of cigarette smoke crowning
Bogart as he winces through it.

You not in the words, not even
Between the words, but a torsion,
A cleavage, a stirring.

You stirring even in the arctic ice,
Even at the dark ocean floor, even
In the cellular flesh of a stone.

Gas. Gossamer. My poker friends
Question your presence
In a poem by me, passing the magazine
One to another.

Not the stone and not the words, you
Like a veil over Arthur's headstone,
The passage from Proverbs he chose
While he was too ill to teach
And still well enough to read, *I was*
*Beside the master craftsman*
*Delighting him day after day, ever*
*At play in his presence*—you

A soothing veil of distraction playing over
Dying Arthur playing in the hospital,
Thumbing the Bible, fuzzy from medication,

Ever courting your presence.
And you the prognosis,
You in the cough.

Gesturer, when is your spur, your cloud?
You in the airport rituals of greeting and parting.
Indicter, who is your claimant?
Bell at the gate. Spiderweb iron bridge.
Cloak, video, aroma, rue, what is your
Elected silence, where was your seed?

What is Imagination
But your lost child born to give birth to you?

Dire one. Desired one.
Savior, sentencer—

Absence,
Or presence ever at play:
Let those scorn you who never
Starved in your dearth. If I
Dare to disparage
Your harp of shadows I taste
Wormwood and motor oil, I pour
Ashes on my head. You are the wound. You
Be the medicine.

## Autumn Quartet

On my birthday

### I

Others are not the medicine for loneliness—
When I was a child, I wanted to be a knight:
Helmeted, living by a noble code
Above the crowd, to serve, to carry a sword
And a shield blazoned with symbolic meanings:
Arrogant and generous like Launcelot du Lac,
The abducted infant and uncompanioned hero.
Did part of me grow up to be a type?—
Those melancholy males who nearly twitch
With yearning for their silver armor, misplaced.
Humorless. Often the inviting lady,
Fatigued by all his brooding, slips away.

### II

But somehow it was also all mixed up
With Washington astride his horse, the ardor
Of Lafayette, the elegant sad jokes
Of Lincoln, who freed the slaves and demonstrated
That Nature's were the only real noblemen:
It was the assassin that craved the coat of arms.
In his mid-fifties, a chevalier of care,
It was heroic to scribble on the train
The speech that disappointed many people:
Too strange, too brief. And then they called it "great."
Solitary in a vivid dream he saw his mourners,
His coffin swagged in bunting, the marble hall.

*III*

Older than Odysseus, older than Leopold Bloom.
Older than number forty-two was—Jack
Roosevelt Robinson—when I watched him crouch
Trembling on the basepath between first and second
With arms extended, taunting the opponent.
And now older than he was the day he died
Depleted by his solitary ordeal,
A public man. In momentary wonder,
I see him burning again, beyond me, playing
A boyish country game in the gaping cities:
Brooklyn, St. Louis, Philadelphia, Boston.
Nineteen-nineteen to nineteen-seventy-two.

*IV*

The heroes of antiquity were taught
By centaurs, ancient creatures who were half
Rational intelligence, half intuition:
Bearded and hooved, all male, a dying race,
Each solitary as the lawless Cyclops,
But pedagogical and bound by nature
To pass their lonely double knowledge on
To such as Odysseus, who learned to tell the story
Of his life, couched in as many lies as needed.
Among the epic bravos, a civic man.
The centaurs showed him truth in fabulation,
In every living city the haunted ruin.

## ABC

Any body can die, evidently. Few
Go happily, irradiating joy,

Knowledge, love. Many
Need oblivion, painkillers,
Quickest respite.

Sweet time unafflicted,
Various world:

X = your zenith.

# An Alphabet of My Dead

In the dark bed, against the insomnia and its tedium, I have told them over many times: a game not morbid but reassuring. Different names each time, but with recurrences.

I tell them over not as a memorial comfort, and not for the souls of the dead, but as evidence that I may be real. Inside the little deerskin medicine pouch flapping at my saddle, these tokens of who I have been. Therefore I exist, sleepless.

.

Harry Antonucci, who used to play basketball at the Jewish Community Center, as many Italian kids did, paying five dollars to join the same way a Jewish boy might find it convenient to join the YMCA.

He was a year ahead of me in school, tall, a good ballplayer although the colored part of one eye was milky dull, skewed away from where his good eye was looking. A sourpuss, swinging his head in an irritable way and too ready to call fouls against himself. In contrast, his graceful, soft jump shot.

The scowl and his swaying walk seemed to express anger at having a bad eye. We made fun of him for being grouchy and for being half blind.

But as we got older he became part of the crowd known as "popular." The night he died, the car he was in and the one right behind it were both full of kids from the senior class: football players, class officers, a blond girl named Cornelia Woolley who was Harry's date. She was bruised and scarred; he was the only one killed.

At first it surprised me that Harry Antonucci would be taking out Neil Woolley. She seemed too popular to be linked with a grumpy, one-eyed Italian who swayed sideways when he walked. But trying to remember him I saw that he had been handsome: fine features, white skin, dark curly hair.

And years after that I realized that a girl could be attracted by that wounded manner, the shadow of a lost eye.

.

B, C, D. Some poets. Elizabeth Bishop. The last time she was in public was at the Grolier Book Shop, at the afternoon signing party for my second book of poetry. Then afterwards, getting ready for dinner, the sudden stroke.

A "good death," fortunate, people called it, but she didn't get to witness the upsurge in her reputation. Nor Cummings the decline in his. Even before I learned about his right-wing politics, the Red-baiting and anti-Semitism, I had come to dislike the person behind the poems that once attracted me. The reliance on charm came to seem grim, unrelenting.

My college friend Henry Dumas, shot dead by a cop in a subway car a few years after graduation. Smart, talented, feckless, a bit of a phony, the first person my age to have a wife and child.

I knew just enough to like him for refusing the Negro stereotypes of the time: communications-major frat boy, street tough, jock. His knit cap, his knowledge of the Bible, his fear as he once explained to me that his wife's father saw through him. His beautiful little boy, a man somewhere now.

Becky Eisenberg, my mother's mother. When she was a teenager she married an older man, a distant cousin, also an Eisenberg. They lived in Arkansas, in a settlement of Jews who had all taken the same last name, that of the rich man from their village in Russia who had succeeded as an American businessman. In that village of Eisenbergs outside Little Rock, Becky gave birth to the older man's daughter, Pearl. Then another cousin, Morris Eisenberg, her own age, came to town on his motorcycle—my grandfather.

When my mother was crazy, Becky, my Nana, took care of me. She was afraid of everything: cars, the mailman, electricity, dogs. Were Nana's terror and her shame rooted in shame she felt for divorcing the first Eisenberg? Or was there any divorce at all?

Morris and Becky left Arkansas together with the child Pearl. My mother, Sylvia, remembers her half sister. She remembers Pearl teaching her how to brush her teeth. Then one day they took Pearl to the station in Baltimore and put her on the train, and that was the last Sylvia saw or heard of her.

It must have been 1922 or 1923. Becky and Morris are dead, probably Pearl, too, and for the story I depend on Sylvia, my mother, who is the spirit of confusion and darkness incarnate. Except for what she says, the story is locked away among the dead forever.

·

Souls, all vaporous mirrors, registers for me of my difference from them. Robert Fitzgerald and Mason Gross, my philosophy teacher—learnèd gentlemen, with the gift of study I have never had. As unlike me as they were, in a different way, Lynda Hull, almost as young when she died as Henry was. Her recklessness of a kind as different from me as Fitzgerald's and Gross's scholarship, the difference producing an oddly similar note of constraint, a cordial awkwardness, when I was with her or one of them.

Drugs, drink. The wistfully lurid movies of her poetry, neon and rain and facepaint, the books and languages of Fitzgerald and Gross. Neighbors to my soul, maybe, but not like my soul.

And another alien mirror, Army Ippolito, football coach and Spanish teacher. When he didn't know what else to do, which was several times a week, he had us sing, *Ya las gaviotas tien' sus alas abren, sus alas para volar. Miles de conchas tien' las 'renas, y perlas tien' la mar!* Or something like that. We used to make fun of Army's way of saying, "It don't make sense."

One day in need of a digression he told the class how when he was young my grandfather, Dave Pinsky, took him to Yankee Stadium. Army got claustrophobia on the subway, became sweaty and panicky, and as Army told it my grandfather was amused and callous, he showed no mercy.

This hardness was a quality Army admired. He considered it a funny story, and I took reflected glory from that, as I believe he intended, which was generous of him. This out-of-it, skinny ineffectual Jewish boy: I knew his grandfather, said Army, he was a tough guy and my benefactor.

And I did learn a little Spanish, one of the few things of the kind I have ever mastered. So in college I read Cervantes and Góngora. Armand, Hippolytus, thank you for that and for your kindness.

A drowsy spell: it is working. Plural dead in categories like counting sheep, the exterminated Jews of Europe, the obliviated Kallikaks of New Jersey, the dead Laborers who framed and plastered these bedroom walls threaded by other dead hands with snaking electrical wires and the dendritic systems of pipes and ducts, audible.

•

Nan M., my high school girlfriend, dead of lung cancer in her thirties. Bill Nestrick, Mrs. Olmstead. Dave Pinsky, the tough guy who took Army Ippolito to Yankee Stadium, and who died of heart failure at my present age—last week, my Aunt Thelma told me that Sylvia, my mother, used to prevent Dave from seeing me. Why?

•

Sir Arthur Quiller-Couch, in the *Oxford Book of English Verse,* 1900, rev. 1939, omitted the stanza of George Gascoigne's "Lullaby of a Lover" in which the sixteenth-century poet refers to his penis. Yvor Winters told me about this omission with great amusement, in 1963. All dead, Quiller-Couch, Winters, Gascoigne, who in his poem does something like what I am doing now:

> Sing lullaby, as women do,
>     Wherewith they bring their babes to rest:
> And lullaby can I sing too,
>     As womanly as can the best.
> With lullaby, they still the child;
> And if I be not much beguiled,
> Full many wanton babes have I,
> Which must be still'd with lullaby.

Quiller-Couch prints the stanzas in which Gascoigne puts to sleep his eyes, his youth, his will, but omits the next-to-last:

> Eke lullaby my loving boy,
>     My little Robin, take thy rest;
> Since age is cold and nothing coy,
>     Keep close thy coin, for so is best;
> With lullaby be thou content,
> With lullaby thy lusts relent,
> Let others pay which hath mo pence;
> Thou art too poor for such expense.

It pleased and amused me to have Winters share this joke on the prudery of Sir Arthur Quiller-Couch. Now, Quiller-Couch has something like a last laugh on us as the opprobrious term "phallocentric" rises on the great wheel turned by the engine of death, always churning, as Gascoigne reminds himself:

> Thus lullaby, my youth, mine eyes,
>     My will, my ware, and all that was.
> I can no mo delays devise,
>     But welcome pain, let pleasure pass;
> With lullaby now take your leave,
> With lullaby your dreams deceive;
> And when you rise with waking eye,
> Remember then this lullaby.

.

Self-destroyers. Carl R., in the eighth grade, the big inoffensive pudgy blond boy who drowned. Jed S., the MIT student who took my poetry class at Wellesley so long ago and presented his poems on long scrolls of computer paper, the all-capitals dot matrix lines nearly unreadable. The first computer printouts I'd ever seen.

They found Jed in his room with a plastic bag over his head, possibly to enhance some drug he had taken. In the MIT literary magazine he published a dialogue between "Socrates" and "S." At the end of this piece, Socrates says, "S., your arguments have refuted me completely—there is nothing more I can say."

T., the graduate student who was caught stealing.

.

U the completely unknown, all the millions like dry leaves whose lives, rounded or cut off in themselves, touched mine not at all.

.

Butch Voorhies, the middle son of the only family that lived in the rooming house next door to us. That miserable neighborhood was stratified: my building housed only families, both buildings allowed only white people. Butch and his two brothers and his drunken father and the mother lived in one large room over the porte cochere of a house full of hard-drinking housepainters, laborers, restaurant workers.

He died in the Navy, some kind of accident. When the father, all but a derelict by then, recognized me in a bar years after Butch died, he asked me to buy him a drink. Maudlin, sentimental, extravagantly dirty. Huck Finn's father.

"Porte cochere" was my mother's word. Once she saw me helping Butch carry home a can of kerosene for their heating stove. He lugged it for ten steps, then I did my ten steps, taking turns all the way from Burroughs' Hardware.

Sylvia scolded me for the friendship. She said the kerosene was to kill the lice on their heads. Keep away from them, said Sylvia, or you'll be covered with vermin.

Then I told her I had seen the stove in that room carpeted everywhere with bedding and clothes, a double hot plate and tiny sink in one corner: the kerosene was for the stove. Now I realize that it wasn't the vermin she feared, precisely, but some worse contagion of poverty or doom.

Mr. Ronald Voorhies, Sr., drunkard, poor provider, surely you too are long dead. I offer you, too, as a sacrifice to sleep.

·

Old Mr. and Mrs. Williams who lived in a velvet shingle house behind those houses on Rockwell Avenue, I thought they had no electricity because the iceman delivered ice for their icebox. With tongs and a rubber pad on his shoulder. He gave us children splinters of ice from the truckbed. Their house, a phantom from another century.

·

X the unknown ancestors of my eight great-grandparents, unseen multitudes who have created my body, thousands of them reaching back into time, tens of thousands, kings and slaves, savages and sages, warriors and rapists, victims and perpetrators.

And also the time-obscured ancestors of this language I write in, the anonymous creators of the music I hear and the machines I use and the musics and machines that made this music, this machine I type at, all the dead fanning back from the apex of this moment to the unthinkably wide fishtail wake of causes.

.

Not YAHWEH but Yetta of *Yetta's Market* on Rockwell Avenue, at the railroad crossing, the little frame storefront tacked onto the frame house. Jerry Lewis invented a song, "Yetta, I'll Never Forget Huh."

.

Zagreus, ancient god of the past, dead one, give me my honey measure of sleep.

## The Haunted Ruin

Even your computer is a haunted ruin, as your
Blood leaves something of itself, warming
The tool in your hand.

From far off, down the billion corridors
Of the semiconductor, military
Pipes grieve at the junctures.

This too smells of the body, its heated
Polymers smell of breast milk
And worry-sweat.

Hum of so many cycles in current, voltage
Of the past. Sing, wires. Feel, hand. Eyes,
Watch and form

Legs and bellies of characters:
Beak and eye of A. Serpentine hiss
S of the foregoers, claw-tines

Of E and of the claw hammer
You bought yesterday, its head
Tasting of light oil, the juice

Of dead striving—the haft
Of ash, for all its urethane varnish, is
Polished by body salts.

Pull, clawhead. Hold, shaft. Steel face,
Strike and relieve me. Voice
Of the maker locked in the baritone

Whine of the handsaw working.
Lost, lingerer like the dead souls of
Vilna, revenant. Machine-soul.

## To the Phoenix

Dark herald, self-conceived in the desert waste,
What *yang* or *yin* enfolds your enigma best?

Memory, whose wing of fire displaces the past—
Or the present, brooding in its ashen nest?

Singing in the flames of Hell, triumphant Christ
Harrowing with Being the Nihil of the Beast—

Or, one foot lifted, one foot planted in dust,
Lord Shiva dancing, hammer in his fist?

You are the emblem of emigrants who crossed
Ocean and continent on their long flight West,

And Entropy's immobile image: chaste
And labile, fluent at rest and saved when lost.

Is time your circle that never comes to rest,
Or the long flight of an arrow Brahma released?

Shakespeare appoints the swan your funeral priest,
The dove your spouse, at rites that you outlast—

Your true counterpart is Speech, the profane ghost:
The quick boy brandishing his lightning-burst.

## A Phonebook Cover Hermes of the Nineteen-forties

Naked but for his wings, unhelmeted,
He flourishes a jagged bundle
Of lightning in one raised fist.

His other hand at his hip grips
A thick sinuous bunch of the cable
That spirals his trunk and legs

Rooted on the North Pole, the sole
Of one foot extending down
Over Alaska, balancing him

Tiptoe on the globe. Gazing
Nowhere in particular, the slender
Thunderer surrounded by thunder,

Fire zigzag in his grasp, labeled "Spirit
Of Communication"—unhistorical,
Pure, the merciless messenger.

# The Cycles

Vilna, "Jerusalem of the North," progressive city
No longer Polish or Yiddish, in motes revenant in Berkeley—
Therapists, altruists, artists of the fresh Twentieth Century:
Wing-shod Hermes guider of dead souls, insufficient one,
Cups in his hands across continents remnant granules and wisps,

Turning in time with lost customs and languages. Kentish,
Anasazi, unknown ancestors massacred or merely lost, nations
Names only yet led by a winged thief, deity of processions,
Inventor of music. In his grip all return as less than molecules—
Particles of energy, cycles, vibrations of his lyre strings.

Sky burial in Tibet, sacred mallets and cleavers open the body
Of the dead for carrion birds, symbols of humility and mercy.
O Vulture, cry, in a land of scarce wood your belly is a holy fire,
Amid rocks, your hunger afloat in air is the only earth,
The grieved body rising through the golden window of that eye.

# Porch Steps

*What are the young lovers?* Two souls,
Which is to say a flowing and a flowing,
Two congeries of shadows, in a garden.

Or congeries of moment, changing shape:
A buoy and an anchor, a roof, an anvil,
A curtain drawn across another curtain

Or else undrawn, or raveled and unraveled.
An interpenetration of lacks and echoes
Like cartoon bees that swarm to make a figure,

Hammer or hypodermic or arrow in air
After the victim. Cupid's cruel arrow. The eyes.
Collaboration itself a third that shadows

Two children playing House. A courtly or bumpkin
Art of the body, curtsy in the dance of wants
And havings, clashes and celebration. The teeming

Molecules that comprise a gas or brick
Passengers in that seeming single body.
*And later?* A congeries of shadows, a house,

The style Queen Anne, each panel of the siding
Varying the surface, the kinds of shingle: Chisel,
Fishscale and Sawtooth, spandrels, each window different,

Curtained and echoed, each porch and privacy
Another shape. Fear of the ending. Children
Shouting. Parts sounding: latch-tongue, strike-plate, hinge,

The interpenetrant echoing of the valves
Of door and window. Oil and paint refreshed
And weathered, care for the caretakers. Motes in sun.

# The Superb Lily

"He burned a great Worlde of Papers before he died,
And sayde, the civick Worlde was unworthy of them;
He was so superb" —the word

Meant *arrogant* once, the absolute of pride.
Presidents summered in my hometown, once,
And famous gamblers endowed

Firehouses: the Phil Daly Ladder and Hose
Survives Lincoln, Grant, Garfield, Jim
Brady and Lillian Russell. Pathos

Of survival, briskness of destruction, works
And place half abolished, that once I willed
Dead. I was young. Longing flows now to what

The heart happily would have destroyed:
The boardwalk's mostly gone, the merry-go-round
With its painted scenes of the National Parks

And calliope has been dismantled and sold.
And once, Winslow Homer chose
In his *Long Branch, New Jersey* to paint belles

On the ocean bluffs, frail parasols
And sashes in the sun. All gone. "Superb Lily"—
A name W. C. Fields might call a lady.

There, we called it *Swamp Lily*:
Swollen perennial, that sucks bogs thirstily
In August, in the droning air.

Short-lived, flamboyant, with back-spread
Purple-dotted flame petals, glandular
Purses on the stamens, gaudy,

Spurned scene of first misery and failure,
My hurt memory now the curator—seed
Of covert aspiration, phoenix of still water.

# Summer in Saratoga Springs

Gallery spindle
And porte cochere. Essex green
Ironwork railing

Girdling a wellhead
Spigot of spring water, tasting of iron
And curative absences.

Miraculous font:
My childhood home come back
In avenues of shingle and spandrel,

Town like my old town
Still was in the fifties, summer
Eyesores and showplaces.

Here as there a racetrack:
Idyll of heartbreak or gain made finite,
Breakfast scrambled eggs

And New York State champagne
(Both a little warm) while watching
Thoroughbreds exercise.

On Broadway, a Hasidic
Prince strolls in his gold-embroidered
Caftan where someone has parked

A vintage Oldsmobile—
My father's. Civic beds of curbside
Impatiens flourish

In the dappled shade:
Apparitional, breezy spirit
Of the eighteen-eighties

Or of the early years
Of a life. Unlikely avenues,
Half-mythical, fountainhead.

## To Television

Not a "window on the world"
But as we call you,
A box a tube

Terrarium of dreams and wonders.
Coffer of shades, ordained
Cotillion of phosphors
Or liquid crystal

Homey miracle, tub
Of acquiescence, vein of defiance.
Your patron in the pantheon would be Hermes

Raster dance,
Quick one, little thief, escort
Of the dying and comfort of the sick,

In a blue glow my father and little sister sat
Snuggled in one chair watching you
Their wife and mother was sick in the head
I scorned you and them as I scorned so much

Now I like you best in a hotel room,
Maybe minutes
Before I have to face an audience: behind
The doors of the armoire, box
Within a box—Tom & Jerry, or also brilliant
And reassuring, Oprah Winfrey.

Thank you, for I watched, I watched
Sid Caesar speaking French and Japanese not
Through knowledge but imagination,
His quickness, and Thank you, I watched live
Jackie Robinson stealing

Home, the image—O strung shell—enduring
Fleeter than light like these words we
Remember in: they too are winged
At the helmet and ankles.

# The Green Piano

Aeolian. Gratis. Great thunderer, half-ton infant of miracles
Torn free of charge from the universe by my mother's will.
You must have amazed that half-respectable street

Of triple-decker families and rooming-house housepainters
The day that the bole-ankled oversized hams of your legs
Bobbed in procession up the crazy-paved front walk

Embraced by the arms of Mr. Poppik the seltzer man
And Corydon his black-skinned helper, tendering your thighs
Thick as a man up our steps. We are not reptiles:

Even the male body bears nipples, as if to remind us
We are designed for dependence and nutriment, past
Into future. O Europe, they budged your case, its ponderous

Guts of iron and brass, ten kinds of hardwood and felt
Up those heel-pocked risers and treads splintering tinder.
Angelic nurse of clamor, yearner, tinkler, dominator—

O Elephant, you were for me! When the tuner Mr. Otto Van Brunt
Pronounced you excellent despite the cracked sounding board, we
Obeyed him and swabbed your ivories with hydrogen peroxide.

You blocked a doorway and filled most of the living room.
The sofa and chairs dwindled to a ram and ewes, cowering: now,
The colored neighbors could be positive we were crazy and rich,

As we thought the people were who gave you away for the moving
Out of their carriage house—they had painted you the color of pea soup.
The drunk man my mother hired never finished antiquing you

Ivory and umber, so you stood half done, a throbbing mistreated noble,
Genuine—my mother's swollen livestock of love: lost one, unmastered:
You were the beast she led to the shrine of my genius, mistaken.

Endlessly I bonged according to my own chord system *Humoresque,*
*The Talk of the Town, What'd I Say.* Then one day they painted you pink.
Pink is how my sister remembers you the Saturday afternoon

When our mother fell on her head, dusty pink as I turn on the bench
In my sister's memory to see them carrying our mother up the last
Steps and into the living room, inaugurating the reign of our confusion.

They sued the builder of the house she fell in, with the settlement
They bought a house at last and one day when I came home from college
You were gone, mahogany breast, who nursed me through those

Years of the Concussion, and there was a crappy little Baldwin Acrosonic
In your place, gleaming, walnut shell. You were gone, despoiled one—
Pink one, forever-green one, white-and-gold one, comforter, a living soul.

# Machines

Leather and brass, wood, forged or die-cut steel.
Silicon, gold electrodes, chased gear, bronze pawl.
Silver wing, Iron Horse. Its hum or wail

Or white noise whispering of molten soul
Poured by makers into the tiny grail
Of escapement at my wrist. Or a roaring bull,

And I astride it, or inside at the wheel:
The animate engine a golem angel flail
Thrashing the germ of spirit from its hull.

Or magnetic speakers, that ape the primate pull
To lip the air, voice matter—the tongue of will
Cleaving the material to its euphoric call.

## Victrola

Dead forty years Bird brings his lips to the reed.
He rules the roost, and rues the rest,
Do wot-jadda bop.

Recovered from shell shock
The war veteran Hitler found the doctor
Who cured his hysterical deafness,

And had the man killed, hoping that I
Might never exist to tell the story here,
A little distorted.

But Illinois Jacquet playing *'Round Midnight*
On the bassoon, better even
Than the death speech of Falstaff.

And listen, Moshe Leib Halpern, I
Have a miracle cabinet
Made in Japan—listen.

# Song

Air an instrument of the tongue,
The tongue an instrument
Of the body. The body
An instrument of spirit,
The spirit a being of the air.

The bird a medium of song.
Song a microcosm, a containment
Like the fresh hotel room, ready
For each new visitor to inherit
For a little world of time there.

In the Cornell box, among
Ephemera as its element,
The preserved bird—a study
In spontaneous elegy, the parrot
Art, mortal in its cornered sphere.

## Steel Drum Variations

Achilles' spear supposedly had the power
To heal the wounds it gave: more awful the weapon—
That threatened anyone it maimed with hope
At the sweet mercy of Achilles. And Time,
Which pushes up the blades of grass from earth
And makes them green, will wither them in winter,
Says Dante, wounding with his gift for words:
And you and your name are like that color in grass—
A thousand years from now, who'll care if you
Lived to your ripeness, or died as a tiny baby
That hadn't learned the words for "bread" or "money"?

We do remember Dante. But Merlin is lame:
When the midwife delivered him, he looked
Up at her, opening his mouth, which had
All of its teeth, and greeted her in Latin—
Terrified, the woman dropped him to the floor,
Which wrecked the infant's hip. The prodigy
In words is monstrous, unlike in chess or music.
Or all earth's children are always maimed or marred:
*Each creature in unconstant mother lieth.*
*The nurse-life wheat, within its green husk growing,*
*Tickles desire with hope of near enjoying.*

Earth smelted, extruded, welded. The ore to iron,
Pig iron to steel. The gouts of sweet crude oil
Fractioned and cracked and measured by the barrel,
The real as well as theoretical barrel,
Drum, ribs, rim, seam, endpiece and fitted bung.

Rusting unlidded eyesore of industrial spaces,
Barren, unpromising stinker, oven of rubble—
Tunable, resonant, the instrument
Of an invented music: percussive squat
Column of darkness, the scooped-out tortoise's shell
Pierced for a lyre and strung with a rabbit's guts.

# The Hall

The hero travels homeward and outward at once,
Master of circumstance and slave to chance.

A spirit old and young, man, woman—each life
A spurt of knowing. The hero is the wife

Stitching all day a story unstitched at night
And also the son who calls the Council to meet

In the beamed Hall where the old ones used to gather.
Differing there, each regards all and each other.

A solitary old chief, the hero grieves
His dead companions, a nation full of lives,

The bird in cold and darkness buffeted in
Briefly through the bright warm hall and out again.

*All nations wither,* Chief Seattle said,
*And yet they are not powerless, the dead.*

The shifting hero wanders alien places,
Through customs of cities and histories of races,

Their arts and evils, their goods, odd works and treasures.
Provincial, cosmopolitan, the hero embroiders,

Recollects, travels and summons together all—
All manners of the dead and living, in the great Hall.

## The Tragic Chorus

Annual festival of the god of reborn souls and abandon,
The young drunken one who dies and in springtime rises:
From all over the City families come to the great amphitheater
With picnics of roast fowl, rounds of bread, cheeses,
Preserved meats, earthen jars of wine and citron water,
Feasting all afternoon on the stadium's grassy terraces
All in civic ease together, witnessing the terrible cadences
Of matricide, fratricide, betrayal, revenge and defiant ambition.

And the show, while religious—the stage is the god's altar—
Takes place as a public competition: eminent citizens
Sponsor the dramas, paying the chorusmaster and writer,
The Chorus shouting and thrusting and retreating in unison,
Their gestures fluid, then stiff, then again fluid, fully
Prescribed as in Yom Kippur, Ramadan or Easter ritual
But also Super Bowl, also highschool tourney or rally
Local as much as divine, the ecstatic piety communal.

And since the tragedy makers the rich men commission
Vie for prizes awarded at the drunk god's festival
It also resembles Academy Awards, Emmys, Pulitzers,
All focused on the City arena—City of slavery, of oppression
Of women willed by their husbands, who got them from their fathers,
As property to their own sons. City of actual sacrifice,
The scapegoat slave crowned with horns. Feel it at the revival,
Train station, ballgame: the breathing public organism.

And the chanting male chorus moves to a military rhythm:
A blind man who desired to join his countrymen in battle

Was able to fight, because he had learned the steps and gestures
Of the squad chanting with interlocked shields braced and flourished,
And the heavy spears with their barbed bronze points gouging
In blind unison, the rhythm one creature's aggregate will, each
Unseeing trusting all to do their part thrusting, keeping time though
You perish in the Chorus: martial, holy, carnival, carnal, the civic art.

## In Memory of Congresswoman Barbara Jordan

Rare spirit hearkened to now with a pang
Of half-forgotten clarity or density:
A quality, quilled, a learnèd freshness

Unshattered though not perfect—not Eden, not
That rippled meander through newborn islands,
Those parentless first leaves and branches tender

And green marsh fresh, the blue, the white feet
Of our adolescent mother, myth of
Perfection imagined just before unperfecting

Itself as if by impulse. And grinning
Cynically in a tree, bearded bignose already
Stuck on his tube of body, the Crawler: we

The tempter, we the corrupted, with no notion
Where bright spirits are culled—our very
Admiration a self-exculpation. "Who

Is this strange bird?" we say as if the
Achieved idea were a sport—like a certain
Parrot, gaudy escapee from some

Domestic cage into azure margins
Of California: crested stranger, it joined
A band of crows, flew and fed with them

Conducting itself as one brilliant
Crow. We prefer that to this other
Realized excellence, eloquence made of our

Same eggs and flowers and waters, plumed
As we are, no feathered exception immune
To that first painted April when we fell,

We fowl of a feather we feel we fail—
And not that she made it look difficult
Or easy but possible—and we fall.

# Biography

Stone wheel that sharpens the blade that mows the grain,
Wheel of the sunflower turning, wheel that turns
The spiral press that squeezes the oil expressed
From shale or olives. Particles that turn to mud
On the potter's wheel that spins to form the vessel
That holds the oil that drips to cool the blade.

My mother's dreadful fall. Her mother's dread
Of all things: death, life, birth. My brother's birth
Just before the fall, his birth again in Jesus.
Wobble and blur of my soul, born only once,
That cleaves to circles. The moon, the eye, the year,
Circle of causes or chaos or turns of chance.

The line of a tune as it cycles back to the root,
Arc of the changes. The line from there to here
Of Ellen speaking, thread of my circle of friends,
The art of lines, chord of the circle of work.
Radius. Lives of children growing away,
The plant radiant in air, its root in dark.

# At the Worcester Museum

That mastery is fiery in the blood
Is nearly imperceptible in us, and yet
We are the animal that snaked the Romex
To junction boxes, that measured and laid
The pipes, that nailed this flooring
And subfloor to the joists and drew the plans.

Inheritors, bored or exalted, we turn
Murmuring through the galleries'
Underwater stillness. What force pressed
Wooden molds into plaster, breath
Into glass, tools into stone or wood,
Moves us through the Muses-house—stunned
By so much striving hung in stillness,
The demonstrated spectacle of collection
And preservation, catalogued. Entropy
Suspended trembles in worn marble stairs.

Here is *Domestic Conflict,* in an ink
So acid it eats away the paper where
The drawing is at its densest, the wife's
Hand turning aside her husband's pistol barrel.

And here the arm of a Meroitic prince
Angles his war axe high above his head
In bas-relief to slay twelve enemies.
They gape their terror while his regal fist
Grips the whole dozen by their gathered hair.
Egyptian his profiled, imperial stance,

Sudanese Kush his features, calm
As any Buddha. Although he died
Before he came to power,
Perhaps a child, whatever spirit
Demands presence in absence
Sculpted the vision of his triumph here.

O long-dead royal infant, memory
Tangles and swerves: twenty centuries
Before the Yankees wangled Massachusetts
From Narragansets and Wampanoags
A Greco-African master hired by your father
Carved female Victory floating
On sandstone wings like the Holy Ghost
To wield her flywhisk at your brow—
Or like memory, the Muses' mother,
Though they are bright and she is dark
As the winged fates the Vikings called
The Wyrds: in collection and recollection,
Elegy and memorial of the dead.

On one wall here in the bathroom
Someone has painted—since painted
Over in the palimpsest of time
And barely visible—a heart and the legend,
*Helio and Marie will fuck forever.*

"Forever." Collection and recollection—
*Memento mori.* Even the motion
Of this Franz Kline, and Bourke-White's silver
Flashes in *Moscow under Air Attack*
Are emblems of the dead,

It's in the shepherdess's skin:
Everyone you love and everyone you know
Will die: we are all a room of skulls
Gazing at these walls. And all our things:
Your garments, your house, your car,
Your animals, your music and mortal pictures.

Worcester eminences, prosperous
Congregationalists and Unitarians:
The third Stephen Salisbury,
Bachelor, last of his family line
Of Yankee dealers. John Chandler
Bancroft, collector of three thousand
Japanese woodblock prints. They made
A temple for the population of the thriving
Mill city, bringing the hive tribute to
Possession—or to Classical, recalled
Leisure and prowess. Immigrant
Children from Cork, Poznan or Piacenza
Saw Miyagawa Chōshun's picture
Of the Floating World: *Amusements*
*At Cherry-Blossom-Viewing Time*:
Sake and music of the samisen.

And still smouldering in memory,
This half-brutal excreted sweetness:
Banging their pans and kettles
Or rattling a stick along a rake
To attract the honeybee
The hooved and heavy-breasted
Sexual creatures of Piero
Di Cosimo's *Discovery of Honey*

*By Bacchus* dance and grin.
One furry-thighed mother
Suckles her faun. Lord Bacchus,
The ever-born prince of pleasure
And violent orgy, hugs Ariadne.

As bees swarm to the tree,
In loud ecstatic procession the monstrous
Yet nearly human celebrants pay
Homage to their languid, immortal lord,
Bacchus the drunkard, great
Breaker of structures—spirit
Of this live remnant that abides
In conservation: this place apparently
Apart, and barely tangent to the real
City outside it: this nearly condescending
Palace, marbled, civic, still, medicinal,
Stuffy or cool, so subtly tiring, that seems
So separate from the world—it is
The world, or what we remember of the world.

# The Knight's Prayer

He prayed in silence.

Even in his personal extreme
Of woe and dread, which was neither
Heroic nor intolerable but sufficiently
Woeful and dreadful, he would not waver
From that discipline.

In his vanity as severely
Logical as a clever adolescent, he found
All vocal terms of sanctity impertinent.

He also rejected gestures: the stagey pose
Of the figure in armor on one knee,
Hands and brow resting on the cruciform hilt
Of a still-scabbarded weapon.
The words and the pose contradicted
Themselves, their conventionality made them
Symbols of worldly attachment.

Therefore in his own prayers he strove
For intimacy, a near-absence of petition.
In his pride he began to abjure even
The request for the strength to ask nothing.

He prayed for steadfastness. In the exploits
He most envied, heroes of old
Endured hardship and ordeals. Worldly
Attachment was their assigned

Burden of imperfection:
Bearing it was their mission.

*Lest these prayers be*
*For weariness of life, not love of Thee,*
He had read: a standard he admired
Not in the name of love
But for its stringency: the gauntlet
Of chainmail not folded
On the breviary, but brandished,
Able for the task.

Then, that abrupt personal extreme
Of woe and dread, neither
Heroic nor intolerable: a cause
To fear the silence. The soul
Stammering to itself.

It was not "In fear of the Lord
Is the beginning of wisdom."

But in fear a new
Model for worldly attachment:

It was like the birth
Of an infant: the father, in sudden
Overthrow, turning from indifference
To absolute care, a ferocity
Of petition dwarfing desire,
All of life flowing at once
Toward the new, incompetent soul.

# Jersey Rain

Now near the end of the middle stretch of road
What have I learned? Some earthly wiles. An art.
That often I cannot tell good fortune from bad,
That once had seemed so easy to tell apart.

The source of art and woe aslant in wind
Dissolves or nourishes everything it touches.
What roadbank gullies and ruts it doesn't mend
It carves the deeper, boiling tawny in ditches.

It spends itself regardless into the ocean.
It stains and scours and makes things dark or bright:
Sweat of the moon, a shroud of benediction,
The chilly liquefaction of day to night,

The Jersey rain, my rain, soaks all as one:
It smites Metuchen, Rahway, Saddle River,
Fair Haven, Newark, Little Silver, Bayonne.
I feel it churning even in fair weather

To craze distinction, dry the same as wet.
In ripples of heat the August drought still feeds
Vapors in the sky that swell to drench my state—
The Jersey rain, my rain, in streams and beads

Of indissoluble grudge and aspiration:
Original milk, replenisher of grief,
Descending destroyer, arrowed source of passion,
Silver and black, executioner, source of life.